Be Gentle with Me, I'm Grieving

Robin Chodak

ISBN-10:0-9987088-0-1

ISBN-13: 978-09987088-0-5

Library of Congress Catalog Card number: 2017902573

Published in the United States of America

Website:www.robinchodak.com

This book is written for all those who have grieved, for those grieving now and for those yet to grieve.

~ Robin Chodak

Table of Contents

ACKNOWLEDGMENTS

An immense thank you to my husband Gerry for the love and support he has given me on my journey through grief. I am grateful for his understanding and love. Without him, this book would not be possible. I am grateful for those who assisted with the editing of this book, Gina Donaldson, Kathy Fontaine, Angie Hamilton and my husband.

INTRODUCTION

How did this book come to be written? The answer is mystical. I was asked to go to a meditation with my friend Cherie on Friday night, 12/6/13. It was much needed because my husband and I had just returned to Florida two weeks prior to our newly renovated condo. Unfortunately, it was not finished and we were living amongst dust, boxes and workers coming and going all day long. I found the situation extremely stressful, so I welcomed her invitation.

The meditation was held at Barbara's house. She suggested we ask angels to come to us, to ask them their names and ask them for answers to any questions we would have for them. Now, just to let you know, I believe in angels but I never really asked them their names or asked them questions. Nevertheless, I decided during the meditation that I would do so. With my eyes closed I entered into deep breathing, then relaxation, then I did indeed ask for angels to come to me if they had a purpose. After a few minutes I saw flashes of white light with my right eye. I asked if this light was an angel and the answer was "Yes." I asked what is your name? "Michael," was the response. At that time I had no questions to ask Michael. I just sat in his presence feeling very calm. I lifted my open hands from my lap about 6 inches high and felt something heavy as if I were holding a large piece of energy. This was a feeling I was accustomed to since I had been certified in Reiki. A few minutes passed and my hands began to open about 12 inches apart. I continued to sit with the energy and then asked Michael, "What am I holding?" The answer wasn't a voice; instead it was an image. I saw in my right-hand that I was holding half of a heart. The inside had jagged edges and it was the color white. I looked to my left hand and I was holding the other half. I asked Michael, "What does this mean?" He responded, "This was your heart. It was once broken and now it is not." As he spoke, my hands moved the two jagged pieces together to create a perfectly whole shaped heart. I felt the presence of peace and asked, "What do I do with this?" He said, "You can help others heal their broken heart just as yours has been mended. That is the reason I have shown you this."

I sat in my meditation several more minutes and asked, "How?"

I waited. And the response was one word. *Write.* Feeling a little annoyed, I began to talk to Michael and said *I am writing*. Don't you know that I have been writing my memoir for five years? I write my Facebook posts weekly. I wrote articles for LOSS (Loving Outreach of Suicide Survivors) and AFSP (American Foundation for Suicide Prevention). I also just wrote a piece for another author who plans to publish a grief book. I'm already writing, I don't understand. I began to feel a little anxious and questioned his validity. I waited and breathed deeply and then felt myself going into a deeper meditation and I heard the word "trust." Then Barbara rang a chime to bring us out of meditation. The 30 minutes had passed and I was still holding up my hands with no feelings of discomfort.

Incredibly, Barbara validated my meditation with her words. First she began to talk about her experiences with her angel named Michael. She has had a relationship with him since the 1990's. Second she spoke about herself being a writing teacher. It made me aware that I needed to trust my own encounter with Michael. When I left I realized that I needed to begin to pay attention to Michael and my inner voice.

Two days later I was in another meditation and I asked Michael, "Why was my heart white?" It never dawned on me to ask earlier. His response, "Your heart was symbolically white and not red because it is no longer bleeding, it is filled with God's white light and love and you can help others." Wow, this was something I couldn't ignore. So here I am beginning a new book. I am glad you are here on this journey with me.

I believe writing down our thoughts is very important during the grieving process. It certainly has been for me. I have compiled a list of questions after each chapter for you to answer truthfully. These questions can also be used in a group setting and open for discussion. Answering them will allow you to take a personal inventory that can help you on your journey. Be honest as you write. Date your answers and go back next year and review what you had written. See if your answers have changed. This is a good evaluation tool to access your progress on your journey of recovery. My thoughts and prayers are with you.

Chapter 1: About Grief and What I have Learned

You may ask why I am qualified to write this book? I don't have a Ph.D and I am not a psychotherapist. But experience is the best teacher and I have had many periods of grief in my life, thus I consider myself well versed on the subject. Mine started when I was a child. My mom and dad had a tumultuous marriage and my dad was rarely home. My mom worked nights as a waitress and I had to take care of my three siblings at the age of 11. I took on the responsibilities of a mother as a young girl; therefore I lost the joys of being a carefree child. I didn't know what it felt like to have sleepovers or go to after school activities or friends' pool parties. There was no time in my life for those things because I needed to be home after school to babysit. I grieved the absence of those childhood years. My parents divorced when I was 13. I felt the loss of my family unit and the finality of it. Realizing my family was broken and could never be repaired created a huge whole in my heart. As a young girl I felt damaged.

The *coup de gras* for my grief was when I became pregnant at 15. My life situation made it easy for it to occur since I didn't have much adult supervision. I don't blame my mother; she did the best she could as she tried to provide for us while working long hours as a waitress. But I carried resentment against my father for a long time. As soon as someone showed me love and attention I gravitated to it. I met John who was almost 18 at a high school dance. He looked cute to me with his cowboy boots, tight fitting jeans and large silver belt buckle. We danced together that night and we continued to see each other. He was nice to me and said he *loved me.* In my mind it made sense to give him what all boys filled with high testosterone desired. I was young and naive and never prepared for the inevitable to happen.

I could not entertain the idea of an abortion, therefore leaving my house seemed to be the ticket I wanted for a new life. John asked to marry me and I agreed. I became a wife and mother at 16. Thankfully, my mom was supportive through it all. I am blessed with a beautiful daughter, yet I grieved the years I missed to discover life and its many experiences as a teenager. Grief cast its dark power on me early in life.

When I was 24, my 16-year-old sister received a diagnosis of bone cancer. I watched the insidious disease suck the life right out of her. It was relentless as it reduced her once strong body to dangling bones. I saw how my mom suffered as she tried to handle things on her own and watch her daughter suffer in pain. I felt hopeless and didn't know how to help them. My sister fought hard, but after four years she finally lost the battle at the young age of 20. I grieved the loss of her and through it I discovered I was full of anger.

After 15 years of marriage John and I divorced. He was a good man, but we grew apart and I felt I needed to experience my life in a new way. I grieved the loss of another broken family even though I knew it was best for me. For most of my life the cloud of grief overshadowed me. I didn't have many coping skills at a young age to process my emotions.

At age 35, I felt that grief had finally given me a reprieve when I met Steve. We fell in love almost immediately and were married eight months later. I know it sounds crazy to marry so soon after meeting someone, but we had a soul connection that the cosmos could not deny. Finally, it seemed my life had started a new course in an upward direction, but sadly after five years of marriage Steve was diagnosed with a rare, incurable cancer. Usually it affected men in their 60's but Steve was only in his 40's. I didn't expect the grief to rear its ugly head so soon. I grieved the loss of our intimate relationship and my dreams of a long life of happiness vanished.

I lived in and out of fear while I watched Steve suffer from the horrendous side effects of the cancer therapies. Everyone expected him to be dead within three years but miraculously five years later he was still alive. I believed we were given a second chance. But then the unthinkable happened. It was not anything that I could have prepared myself for and it didn't make sense. Even if I had developed strong coping skills, had a Ph.D in psychotherapy or read every self-help book to prepare me for what was to come they would not have helped. I came home from work to find my beloved husband dead on our basement floor from self-inflicted gunshot wounds to his head. It was the most tragic event in my life and I thought I would never recover. But I have survived and it is the reason I am writing this book 11 years later. My life with Steve and my journey to recovery are discussed in greater detail in my memoir. Perhaps without those grief experiences I would not be the person I am today nor have changed in positive ways.

I am not alone in my grief. Thousands are suffering daily due to many tragedies, losses and especially suicide. At the time of this writing the most recent data in the U.S. reported by the Centers for Disease Control states 41,149 suicides in 2013. In that year someone died by suicide every 12.8 minutes. How are those who have lost their loved one surviving? The answer is not so easily. Many are falling prey to prescription drugs and alcohol to ease their pain. Our culture and beliefs about grief do not support the griever fully.

Based on my experiences with grief I can say that death by suicide is like none other. The only way to describe it is to be vulgar and say, "It sucks." And those that say "get over it" have no clue about what is really going on within us. In fact they say it because they are in denial. Grief is painful and who really wants to suffer? It is not something we chose to inflict upon ourselves. It usually gives no warning and suddenly jumps on its victim like a hungry wolf. The only way to resume your life in a healthy way after you have lost someone you loved is first to deeply grieve. This applies to everyone, not only suicide survivors.

Over the last 11 years since Steve's suicide in 2005, I have worked on my own grief and have observed others in their grieving. It has not been a welcomed or pleasant process. On the contrary, it has been the most challenging journey of my life and I believe many of you reading this could say the same about events that have happened in yours. When I hit bottom I knew I had two choices. Either I could stay in the debilitating state I was in or I could begin to change my thinking. I chose the latter and because of it I have a new perspective. I chose to view and live my life differently.

How did I get to a place of serenity and peace? That is always the number one question asked and there is not an easy answer nor is the explanation an exact science. It is a process. It takes time and there are things that you must do and continue to do. The most important thing is don't deny your grief. You must realize that you are the one who holds the power *not* grief. What I have discovered and have always said is: "Grief can either be your friend or your enemy. It is your friend when you take it by the hand and walk through it together. It is your enemy if you deny it exists and run from it." Running away makes grief mad and it will try to strangle you tighter. So, how can you make it your friend? A true friend would want the best for you. Grief wants this for you too. It wants you to recover and become stronger but only when you process it. You must not try to escape it. In order to do that you must acknowledge your loss.

I needed to acknowledge that Steve chose to end his life by shooting himself in the head two times in our basement. Initially, I denied it. I believed someone had murdered him. It wasn't very far fetched to think it since he was involved in politics. I couldn't imagine he would ever hurt himself or me. I had to come to terms with the choice *he* made. It wasn't *mine;* it was *his.* As we evolve we must do this in all aspects of our lives.

Next, I needed to accept that he was dead by suicide. Not from cancer and not from natural causes, but by his own hand and I had to live with the stigma associated with it. Dying from cancer or natural causes would have been acceptable, but not suicide.

There was nothing I could do to bring Steve back, not my wishing, hoping, grieving, or praying. I realized I needed to begin to allow myself to grieve. I had to acknowledge the feelings I experienced such as anger, sadness, loneliness and guilt. This takes work because our society doesn't support us in the process. I had to learn that it was all right to feel anger toward Steve for leaving me. It also was OK to feel anger toward God. For some reason I didn't think God could handle it or I was afraid to express it. I know now that it was healthy for me to feel it and OK for me to yell and scream at God. He could take it and strangely by my doing so I felt connected to His power. It was the same power that kept me going, it always picked me up when I fell down. Keeping our emotions bottled up inside does not allow us to start the journey of recovery.

The next thing to do is make choices to move forward and not stay stuck in the defining moment that changed our lives. Too many times we remain in the awful dark place due to feelings of guilt and never find happiness again. So many people cannot pick up the pieces and begin to live their lives after this type of tragedy. They have lost sight that their life is a precious gift and meant to be lived with fulfillment. Grief has a bag full of tricks and that is only one that it plays on a sorrowful heart. It wants to rob you of the belief that your life has meaning and purpose.

Survivors feel guilty that they did not stop the suicide. Are we psychics or mind readers? We tell ourselves we should have known or we could have prevented it by changing our path that day. That type of thinking is harmfully wrong. We cannot control anyone else's behavior or actions, only our own. The "what if" questions haunt survivors and can halt us in our recovery tracks if we let it.

Our society as a whole is uncomfortable with grief. People don't know how to handle it and when they see us in distress they don't know what to do or say. If I could give advice to them I would say, "Please, let us feel what we are feeling." We should not feel that we must stuff our grief inside our pants and belt it up as if it never existed to protect those who are uneasy about it. Doing that is the worst behavior for the grievers. We want others to give us permission to feel our feelings of loss, but so many don't allow us that luxury. Why? Because either they have never experienced it and don't understand it or if they have, they never grieved themselves.

We should never pass judgment on a person who is hurting. Pain is pain and we should not minimize the extent of it. Our society needs to be more cognizant of the grieving process and we must be gentle with one another. It may take a longer period of time for one person than it does for another to get to a place of acceptance. Each of us is wired differently and we will experience the grieving process in our own way. As a society we need to learn how to respect the griever and that is the reason I have created a button that reads, "Be Gentle with Me, I'm Grieving."

If someone saw the button they would become aware that the person is experiencing deep pain and maybe they could show compassion in that instant. I think it could be especially helpful for those we do business with or just strangers we come in contact with in our everyday life, such as at the store, bank, dry-cleaners, etc. For example, let's say that soon after your loss you are in the grocery store and the person in the line behind you is annoyed because it is taking you an unusually long time to unload your groceries. Their normal response would be a negative gesture or comment. The thought probably never entered their mind that your loved one died by suicide recently. They don't realize that it took you a great amount of courage to get yourself out of the house. And they simply don't understand that everything a grieving person does takes longer.

Many people don't understand that grievers feel that they are the characters in a silent slow motion film; it is hard for them to get their thoughts together and even move around. It is as if time has stood still for them. Everything has slowed down and many days they can't get themselves out of bed. It is a big deal for them to get to the grocery store because their lives have been changed abruptly with no warning and it takes time for the griever to begin to find their way back to living. If someone saw them wearing the button hopefully it would induce a positive reaction. They may even offer to help unload the groceries or give them a smile. They may also examine their own situation and feel gratitude that they are not the one grieving a loss themselves. I believe as human beings we need to show grace to one another, especially during times of loss.

Another time the button could be useful is in traffic. It seems traffic jams can easily ignite hostility. It includes hand gestures, yelling profanities and angry looks. If a situation occurs that you had no intention of creating, you could hold up the button and wave to the person. If they read the button, it may also change their behavior.

Another example is when a person is at a large gathering and something triggers them to cry. Unable to withhold the tears they could instantly put on the button. They wouldn't need to hide the tears and others would understand. It's as simple as that, no questions asked. There are many other situations where the button could be helpful. It is not intended as a cop-out or to give you license to abuse your power in any way, instead it is a tool. I believe it could begin to reframe how our society reacts to grief and could benefit us all.

Grief defined by freedictionary.com is: "Deep mental anguish, as that arising from bereavement, or an instance of this. A source or cause of deep mental anguish." If grievers experience deep mental anguish why doesn't our culture give them time to recover? Every society has its own mourning rituals. In Western culture black is worn during a funeral and wake. Jewish people sit *Shiva*, which lasts for seven days. These observances are short lived. Why can't we have the luxury to mourn beyond the defined time? There are days when you may feel an intense emotion from your grief and that is the day you can put on your button. Perhaps, it would be the birthday of your deceased or a day that holds a special memory or a holiday. Whatever the reason is, once you put on the button it will allow you to go about your day and feel safe as people become aware of your pain. If we are allowed this luxury, society can take notice and be gentle with us and it will help get us through one more day. This could be a new ritual that we develop. It is not something that is imposed on us nor do we impose it on others.

We can put on our button when needed and all we ask is to be treated with kindness and understanding. An outwardly public display is beneficial and used in other situations such as breast cancer. A woman wears a pink ribbon to create awareness of the disease. A blue ribbon is for men with prostate cancer. Both have national days allocated to acknowledge them. Why can't it be the same for us? We deserve it too! I believe this would begin to change the way we view one another because no one escapes grief during their lifetime.

Questions:

1) What have you learned about grief? Describe it in a few sentences.
2) Have you noticed how others grieve? Can you list some of the ways you observed them grieve over your loss or their own?
3) List all the events in your life that caused you to grieve.
4) Did you have events where you didn't grieve when you should have? List them.
5) Can you accept that you didn't grieve and then let it go?
6) Can you think of situations where putting on the button could have helped? List them.
7) Do you think the button will help others you know? If yes, then buy them one. Let's begin to make the change.

Chapter 2: Stay Connected

Sadly, there are people who think you should just "get over your loss" and "move on." This is a form of denial and will cause problems later on if the anger, guilt, depression, etc., are not dealt with appropriately. If we do not have a chance to recover how can we be a benefit to others in society? I believe we need an awakening and a shift in our thinking about it. We must not stuff down our grief; we must face it and work it. If we try to logically trudge our way through it there will not be lasting results. We need to feel it, understand it and accept it and then make a choice to move in a forward direction without the physical existence of our loved one.

First of all, I want to be clear about this; you can never "get over" the loss of a loved one who died by suicide or tragically. They were a living, breathing person that intertwined their life with yours and your existence will always feel their abrupt absence. What we can do is begin to find ways to keep them alive in our lives. Although we do not have a physical experience with them we can still have a relationship with them. What I mean by that is we can hold our dearest memories of them that bring us joy and we can talk about them. So many people never want to bring up their names because they think it will be too difficult for us. But the truth is we want to talk about them. We don't want to forget them and we don't want our friends and family to either. It seems society wants us to put our memories to rest just as the body decomposes, but we want our memories of them to be present with us.

We can also create rituals to honor them such as light a candle on a day that holds special meaning for us, play the music they liked, talk to them or any other way that is meaningful to us. I believe this keeps them closely connected to our hearts.

I don't believe that the energy of our loved one ever dies. It remains with us always. I also believe they try to communicate with us in various ways, but out of fear we push them away. Not deliberately. It makes sense we don't encounter them often or at all because they cannot exist in our realm of fear and pain. Theirs is only one of peace and they are vibrating at a higher level. If we could sit in a meditative silence abandoning our fears we may get to encounter them in a new way. I believe that they do want to commune with us but we don't understand it. I know Steve has caught my attention in several ways. One was when a Beatles song played on the radio. The first time I heard one after he died it was too painful to listen to so I turned it off. But as time went on I longed to hear the Beatles because I knew how much Steve loved their music. I began to notice that the songs spontaneously played when something had triggered a memory of Steve. Instead of turning the radio off, I listened and began to feel a presence that was foreign to me. It was not frightening; instead it was full of warmth and peace. I believed it was Steve. I didn't physically see him or touch him, but I knew he was near and sensed his energy.

Another way he wanted to communicate with me was through the number 1. Those who study numerology have much to say about the vibrational power of numbers and their meaning. After Steve died I constantly saw 11:11 on the clock and other devices. I had no doubt it was him because we were married on 11:11, plus Steve's life path number is 1. It was his way of letting me know he was around me in an energetic form. I know that many have had much more profound experiences with their deceased loved ones. We should not judge others' encounters. I believe having a continuing energetic bond with them will keep us in a state of peace and awareness of the depths of our love. It keeps us on the road to healing.

Many people don't understand what a grieving person is experiencing and they say things without really knowing how their words affect us such as: *it has happened for a reason, time heals all wounds, they are in a better place, they are no longer suffering, God has a plan, God doesn't give us more than we can handle, this too shall pass, I guess God needed another angel.* And so on. Many of those words were said to me and they certainly didn't bring comfort. Instead they made me resent the person who said them, feeling that they just didn't get it. I am sure you have heard those and others that were not thought out before they were spoken.

Another example not related to suicide is when I heard a woman speak about losing her entire home in a forest fire. She didn't lose a loved one, yet understandably she felt an extreme loss. Someone made the comment, "You must feel so much lighter not having anything." It made sense to the woman who said it because she lived the *Zen* life, but not to the woman who was grieving. That is a perfect example of someone not thinking before speaking. The woman who lost her home could have benefited from wearing my grief button. I don't believe people say hurtful things with malicious intent. They truly are not in touch with grief and don't understand it.

I have come to realize that suicide makes people feel awkward and they can't begin to understand how to process what we are experiencing. It is best for us to let their words roll off our shoulders and keep ourselves from getting angry or resentful. At some point we may say those same things to ourselves such as, *he or she is no longer suffering*, and we have the right to say them when we are ready. Others should not be saying them to us. The most comforting words to me were, "I am here for you" and "I love you." Our hearts have been broken and shattered to pieces and we often don't love ourselves or feel lovable to others after the suicide. The assurance that we really are loved helps us. When Steve died, I initially thought he didn't love me as much as I thought he did, because if so he wouldn't have killed himself. I also thought that I must not have loved him enough. I felt that my love should have kept him alive. But the truth is that it was not about love, it was about pain. His pain. He suffered and couldn't find a way to end it, so he did what he thought was his only choice.

Grief comes to us from many sources. An example of misunderstood grief is a story of my close friend whose cat had died. She lived alone and her cats were like children to her. She bonded with them and experienced the unconditional love that many do from their pets. When she lost one of them she felt no one really understood her loss so she went to a pet support group. She said she felt people were more open about their feelings for their pets than for humans. My friend had experienced many other losses in her life; one being a murder of someone she loved so she certainly knew about grief. She felt that the pet support group was more expressive. I think it proves that our society is still uncomfortable with the grieving process. I hope that it will change over time as more of us begin to express ourselves freely and put on our buttons. Bereavement groups and Facebook pages such as mine (www.facebook.com/recovernowfromloss) are also helpful aids to offer support.

I have learned through my own experiences and from others that grief is very personal and we should not judge each other. I was glad to be available for my friend when she needed an ear to express her thoughts. That is all she really needed and wanted anyway. It was important that her feelings were validated and that is what I did for her. We should learn to do that for each other because none of us will escape losing someone we love at some point in our lives.

Often times others want to fix things for us because they don't know what to do and want us to "move on" quickly. The problem with that is we can begin to become dependent on them and don't learn to trust our own emotions. It is OK to have others around in the beginning, but eventually we must let them go and learn to stand on our own.

As the years pass after our loss we may feel that we have come to a good place and unfortunately when we least expect it another whammy can hit us. That recently happened to me when a dear friend who was too weak to talk, texted me and said she was going into hospice. She said she was ready to make her transition and knew I would understand and to spread the news to our friends. There was nothing more the doctors could do for her after a four-year battle with colon cancer so she chose to get herself *ready* and wait.

I now believe that my husband was *ready* too, otherwise he would not have taken his life. He had been diagnosed with cancer five years before he died and had undergone intense chemotherapy, radiation and a bone marrow transplant. At the time of his death he had no evidence of disease, but I can only speculate that he didn't want to *wait* for the cancer to strike him again and then *wait* for the inevitable. Hearing my friend Mary's news caused the grief that I had processed for years to fall on me like a ton of bricks. If I had that button, "Be Gentle with Me, I'm Grieving," I would have put it on because I was not going to just "get over it." The emotions that I thought were at bay came rushing in and I remembered all the fear and pain I experienced when Steve died. Mary had bravely battled her cancer and I thought she was going to beat it. Perhaps I was in denial because I didn't want to face another loss. All I could do for her was to pray that her transition to the next realm would be easy and pain free.

At moments like those we feel very helpless because we are not able to provide comfort or hope. But I do believe there is tremendous power in prayer, therefore I prayed for her family and friends. I imagined that Mary would experience pure joy in her new home. It is those of us who are left that suffer the pain. After Mary announced that she was going into hospice I knew the inevitable would occur very soon. During those nine days I meditated and prayed and had the chance to tell her via text messaging how much she meant to me, which was a gift. I felt grateful that I could tell her I loved her and she told me she would communicate with me as a hummingbird. I did not get the chance to do that with my husband Steve and I felt intensely cheated.

A few days after Mary's death I decided to go golfing with some friends. I thought that it would be good for me to get my mind clear and give myself a break from my sadness. If you are a golfer you know that nothing should be on your mind but your game and your current golf shot. After playing a few holes I realized that golf was not what I wanted or needed. I swung horribly, my energy was zapped and all I wanted was to be alone. Because I had learned self-care over the years it was easy for me to excuse myself and cancel my plans for the evening. I went home and listened to meditation tapes. After two hours I felt much better and realized that is what I had needed. I remained in the silence all evening and woke refreshed and grateful that I had a chance to communicate with Mary before she died. It is important to not continue to push ourselves when we need to rest; we must learn to listen to our inner voice. A few days later I received a card in the mail from another friend with a picture of a hummingbird on it and I knew Mary was near and at peace.

Unfortunately those of us who have lost our loved one to suicide didn't have the luxury to say our good-byes or pray for them before their parting. I cling to the belief that they are experiencing pure bliss and that we will one day share it with them. My belief brings me comfort and has helped me on my journey of recovery.

As I walked through the years of grief my thoughts continued to change and my eyes continued to see new possibilities for my life.

Questions:

1) Have you felt that others wanted you to just *get over it*? Write down on a piece of paper those situations.

2) List ways you denied your grief.

3) List ways to keep the memory of your loved one alive.

4) List the people you felt didn't understand your grief.

5) Can you come up with any reasons why they misunderstood your grief?

6) Can you forgive them? If you have forgiven them write "forgiven" next to their name on your list. If not write, "I need to forgive." Use this as a guideline for the coming year to make it your goal. Reflect on your answers the following year and if you have not forgiven someone then repeat the step.

Chapter 3: How did this Happen?

A question that is asked by those left behind when a loved one has died by suicide is *how did this happen*? We never expected them to do what they did, *actually take their own life.* Even if they exhibited signs of depression we never imagined the unthinkable. Dying from suicide is unnatural so why should that be on our minds? In my situation and others I have spoken to, we were told by our loved one to never worry about that happening to them. Even after my husband had been admitted to the hospital for having suicidal thoughts he assured me that he would never do anything like *that.* I believed what he told me and I trusted him. Why shouldn't I? He was a trustworthy man and one of faith. He didn't just *talk the talk* he *walked the walk* and exhibited a strong faith. We both believed that God was the giver and taker of life. We were deacons at our church and I never imagined the unthinkable could happen to my husband. *I thought* "Men of God" don't kill themselves. It wasn't conceivable to me that a man who believed in God would ever do anything to harm himself. Unfortunately, I didn't know the depth of my husbands suffering because he hid it from me so well. I don't believe it was because he wanted to be deceptive. Instead, I believe that he wanted to protect me and wasn't in touch with his own feelings.

Our loved ones didn't do what they did to make us suffer; they ended their life because they didn't want to live with their pain any longer. I don't believe they intentionally wanted to hurt us. On the contrary, I think Steve hid his pain from me because he didn't want me to worry. In many cases the depression is so deep that the person is not in touch with their own feelings and it is impossible to express them. They didn't have enough coping abilities available at the time to help them see things differently. That is the difference between them and us; despite how down we may feel during our grief we still have coping mechanisms to put us back on the right path. But they lost their ability to think logically. I believe that Steve's brain didn't function the way it once did before the cancer struck him. He had endured intense chemotherapy and radiation that had changed him in many ways and probably also affected his brain.

I don't believe we will ever know the reason why the tragedy happened to any of us; we can only speculate. I often wondered if Steve had survivor's guilt. I have read that those who have made it through a life threatening disease or tragic accident when everyone else has died from it feel guilty that they survived. I hope that I get the chance to ask him when I join him in the next realm but by then it may not matter anyway. Perhaps there is no memory of this life when we are transitioned to the next. It really doesn't matter but I do like entertaining the idea that I will be able to ask Steve some questions.

It is very easy for those of us left behind to torment ourselves with the questions that can't be answered. We don't know why a loved one was in a place at the exact moment when a tragic accident occurred or why they ended their life. We can fabricate our own ideas and we do so to ease the pain or use them as an excuse. But this will keep us in a stuck state. The truth is we will never know, therefore we must get to a healthy place of acceptance. When we do then we can move forward in our lives, otherwise it is very easy to become a victim of the torment. I know this to be true because I lived in that confusion for a time. The only way to release those feelings is to change our thoughts. We need to let go of the thoughts that bind us so tightly in chains.

Steve's suicide has caused me to think much more deeply about the dying process and also about living. I believe that the physical body dies and is no longer with us but the person's energy can't die. That is a fundamental principle of science; energy cannot be created or destroyed, only transformed. Most human beings fear death and I did too, but I don't any longer. I truly believe that there is another existence in a realm that we don't understand and it will be beyond our wildest dreams. When we get to that place we will probably ask ourselves, *why did we have such fears about it?* Things we don't understand often create fear. I have learned to keep my mind open to all possibilities.

Questions:

1) How many times did you ask yourself, *Why did this happen*?

2) Did asking it over and over again change the answer?

3) Have you been able to stop asking the question?

4) If so, how has it changed you?

5) Have your thoughts on the death experience changed? Write them out.

6) Have your thoughts on living your life changed? Write them out.

Chapter 4: The Shock

When you first discovered that your loved one had died by suicide or suddenly with no warning you may have fallen into a state of shock. It is an understandable reaction. Some become traumatized and suffer from Post Traumatic Stress Disorder. When I found my husband dead I literally dropped to the floor in shock. In that moment my life was forever changed and yours was too when you found out about the suicide of your loved one. I felt I had nothing more to live for without my husband, my soulmate, and the man with whom I intertwined my life. Those feelings are normal and we should seek help from psychotherapists, support groups or grief coaches if we can't process our grief.

Suicide is like no other form of death because it is self-induced, sudden and unnatural. I personally understand the differences because of my sister's death from cancer. After her diagnosis I knew that the possibility of her death existed even though she was only 16 years old. She suffered for four long years of her life. It was tragic for our family when she died, but in a sense it was expected because of her illness. You may think you can prepare for the death of a loved one who is ill, but the truth is that grief still visits and wants to do its time with you. The only difference is that our minds can logically understand death from an illness and not so easily from suicide. Any sudden death brings to us the shock factor.

I have a friend who learned about her only child's death on the news July 17, 1996. Her daughter was traveling on TWA flight 800 from New York to Rome when the plane exploded and crashed into the Atlantic Ocean. All 230 passengers on board were killed. It was the third-deadliest aviation accident to occur on U.S. territory. Hearing about it from the T.V. caused my friend intense grief and also fear that her daughter's body would never be found. Fortunately it was, which did help put that fear to rest. She has had to work very hard on her recovery. When I met her for the first time I would have never imagined such a tragedy occurred in her life. She is a beautiful soul who enjoys her life to the best of her ability. My own mother does too. These women are inspirations to all of us. They do not let their tragedy define them and they have found peace in their lives. I am grateful that my mom passed her strength on to me. I have tremendous respect for all who can survive tragedies in their lives and I am one of them!

I recently made a new friend in a spiritual group and learned that her mother had killed herself over 50 years ago. At the time my friend was 11 years old. I can only imagine how hard it must have been for her at that time when help was much less available as compared to today. There were no support groups, no Internet to hear about other people's experiences and few medications to help with coping. The word *suicide* was barely spoken and if so it was behind closed doors. My friend lived with shame and never talked about it until recently. In the past whenever she was asked on medical forms what was the cause of her parents' death she always lied. There was stigma then and there is still stigma today, which makes it so very difficult for the survivors. We need to talk about our feelings and be allowed to grieve.

If you were the one to find your loved one dead or when you heard the news it is easy to understand your state of disbelief. It immobilizes and causes you to question everything that you once held to be true in your belief system. I had to re-evaluate everything I thought I believed. It led me down a new path in my life and one that I can now say I am grateful to have found. I may not have changed to this degree in the absence of extreme suffering. I shall never know, but I can say that I am happy where I am in this moment.

Questions:

1) Did you experience shock? Write down the emotions you experienced and how your physical body reacted to hearing about or finding your loved one dead by suicide.

2) How long did those symptoms last?

3) List what you did to relieve those symptoms.

4) Which of those symptoms still exist?

5) List ways you can relieve them now.

6) Did your belief system change in any way since your loss?

7) List the things that you no longer believe in that you once did.

8) List things you believe in since your loved one died that you didn't before his or her death.

Chapter 5: The Emotions: Anger, Denial, Depression, Loneliness, and Guilt

The emotions you encounter during the grieving process may seem foreign to you, especially if you have never had any type of loss prior to the suicide. Grief takes you into a realm that is unfamiliar. I had always been hopeful even in the midst of bad circumstances but I took on a whole new persona as I grieved my husband's suicide. I became negative, depressed and hopeless. This was not the person I had always been but grief tried to trick me into believing that I was always that type. If we don't understand the grieving process it can easily destroy us.

I learned first hand that grief was my friend when I didn't deny my feelings. It was my enemy when I tried to run and hide from them. We must get in touch with our emotions and accept them but it takes time, help and effort. Are you willing to travel down that road? If not, then you will find yourself stuck and unable to move forward. The choice is really up to you. No one can force you to start your journey of recovery. You must come to realize that life is meant to be lived to its fullest potential.

At some point during your grief you must shift your thinking to move forward. Many times people feel that the world dumped on them and all they had tried to accomplish meant nothing. They feel that life has been robbed from them and it has nothing else to offer. That is another lie of grief and that way of thinking will keep you stuck. You must change your thoughts 180 degrees to begin your journey. You can see yourself as a victim or instead you can see yourself as a survivor. Begin to envision yourself as someone who can grow stronger and become a better person because of the experience.

After the shock wore off, I went through the many stages of grief; anger being one that was high on the list. The trauma immobilized me and I knew I needed help and found a suicide support group. My anger was so intense that I became angrier knowing that I needed to be in such a place. I was angry at God, angry with my husband for leaving me, angry with myself and angry at the world. As time passed I realized I was not alone and became grateful that I had the support group to express my feelings and I knew it was necessary for me to let go of any anger that held me captive. Many want to sit with their anger and never move forward. If you do that, eventually it will turn you into someone that you no longer recognize. Do you want to look in the mirror years later and see yourself as an unhappy, bitter person? It could happen if you allow it. The best way to avoid it is to find someone you trust to express your emotions and then learn the process of *letting go.* Sometimes you may just need to scream and other times you may want to punch a pillow. Do what you need to do without injuring others or yourself but don't let it make you a prisoner. You will never be the person you were before the tragedy hit, but you must guard against becoming an angry, bitter, unhappy soul. If you want to find peace and happiness you must release those emotions.

Denial is a very common emotion that we experience from a tragic loss. It is easy to live in its realm and run from the truth to avoid pain. I wanted to stay locked in my house and make believe that the tragedy never happened. As if dealing with the suicide wasn't enough, I also had to deal with the media, which complicated my grief even more. Steve's suicide was published in our local paper and the Chicago Sun-Times because he held political positions at the state and local level. The news media loves to create stories about anything they can without understanding how others may be affected and they did just that with me. They didn't realize that their story made my suffering worse since they plastered Steve's face on the front page of the paper. It made me afraid to leave my house and it became my prison for many weeks. I feared being recognized and questioned about the suicide. If I had my button then I would have put it on. It would have given me a sense of security to know that people would be cognizant of my pain and perhaps cautious of their words. I eventually had to walk out of my house without it. And yes, some people said things to upset me. I don't believe they intended it, but it still hurt. I remember one incident at Starbucks when a politician that knew Steve came up to me and began talking about how difficult it was to fill the empty position. The statement in itself was not offensive, but I felt he was treating Steve as just another seat in politics and didn't understand he was a man I loved and lost. I couldn't begin to think about politics or *his* problems. It triggered all the questions that haunted me that I had tried to shut out. This is another example of a situation where the button may have helped. Perhaps he would have been gentle after reading it.

Gossip and bad news travels fast and since Steve's death made the papers it was very likely that most people in my village and in the political circles knew what happened to him. I wondered what they thought.

Did they think we had a bad marriage or that Steve had problems with his children? I didn't know what judgments they made but I certainly didn't want to be interrogated by anyone. The papers also disclosed the gory detail that Steve pulled the trigger not once, but twice, which I didn't know. That knowledge induced more painful thoughts. I wondered if after the first shot he had time to re-evaluate and wish that he hadn't done it. Or did he suffer so much that he had no choice but to pull the trigger a second time? I wondered how long he remained conscious before he died. I hated that those thoughts even entered my mind and I anguished over them. I learned to rely on my own inner strength given by God.

Many survivors become depressed after the suicide even if they haven't had prior symptoms of it, which is understandable. Any emotion we initially feel should never be considered abnormal. It only becomes a problem if it lingers and begins to control our life or causes harm. If that is your case then it is necessary for you to get outside help. The realization that my husband was never coming back caused me to fall into a depressed state. I wondered how I could manage without him. I didn't know where to begin and felt inept in all things. I didn't think that I had anything to live for without the man whom I entangled my life. I had waited for him for 35 years and we only had 10 together. It was too short and I began to have serious thoughts about ending my life so I could join him. Even in the throws of grief my mind still found its way to logical thinking to convince me that suicide was not the answer. Sadly my husband and your loved one didn't have the ability to think rationally.

My thoughts frightened me and I sought out psychotherapy, which started me down my road to recovery. As survivors we need to accept that our life will never be the same and we need to find ways to survive on our own. When one's life is wrapped so intimately with another the grief of separation is intense and you don't believe you will survive. But I am a testimony along with many others that it is possible. It begins with hope and it continues by making healthy choices for your life.

Depression is seductive and it can sneak its way into your life and keep you stuck in your grief if you don't recognize what it is doing. I know several people who needed anti-depressants after the suicide and that is OK; it was temporary and it helped get them on their path of recovery.

I believe that guilt is the most destructive, unproductive emotion that we experience from suicide loss. We don't experience it the same with other types of death because it is understood that we can't control those, such as terminal illness or old age. But with suicide we take on the belief that we somehow could have prevented it if we had done something differently. We often feel that we didn't do things right for them because if we did they would not have killed themselves. But this is a seductive lie that binds us.

Guilt is nasty and it wants to make us suffer. Guilt wants to punish. So what do we do? We continue to punish ourselves for the suicide. What does punishment do to us? It causes us pain. So we live in it because we are allowing guilt to control us. We must have no part of it. We did not cause the suicide nor could we have stopped it no matter how much or little we loved the person or what we did or didn't do for them. It was their choice not ours. We need to understand that we are not to blame. For me, that was the hardest concept to accept. Some us of carry more guilt than others and I believe it becomes inbred in us from our childhood. Oftentimes our parents or religion injected the venomous guilt while we were young and we never found the antidote for it, therefore it makes the suffering of suicide loss even harder on us.

Guilt tricked me into believing that if I had stayed home from work that day the suicide would not have happened. I realized later that I could not stay home everyday. If Steve didn't do it that day, he could have found another one to do it. After going to a support group week after week it finally resonated with me when I heard others say it was their choice. My therapist helped me work on my unresolved issues from my past that had magnified my guilt about Steve's death. Once I truly believed that I was not the guilty one I felt much lighter and could work on all the other negative emotions. Guilt has a way of keeping its victims in an unhealthy place. Survivors must let go of it in order to move forward.

Questions:

1) Did you consider grief your friend or your enemy?

2) List things you can do to make grief your friend.

3) List the emotions you felt initially after your loss.

4) List them after 3 months, 6 and 9 months.

5) List the one emotion that took control over you, i.e. guilt, anger, fear, etc.

6) Does it still control you today and do any others? List them.

7) List how you will release those negative emotions.

Chapter 6: Loss of Identity

When we have lost someone we love we often lose our sense of identity. It doesn't matter what relationship you had with the deceased, you feel that a part of you has died and you no longer know who you are without them. This is a normal reaction in the beginning of the grieving process and I knew exactly how it felt. I was no longer a wife and all the married roles I played no longer existed. If you are a parent who lost a child, you no longer play that role for the deceased son or daughter. You may have other children, but each relationship is different and you still feel the loss of how you identified with that child. If you have lost a sibling you may feel that you have lost your best friend. They may have been your inspiration or someone who always looked out for you. If you have lost your spouse you may feel that you will never find another or you worry about how your children will be without their parent. If you have lost a parent, you may believe that your family has been destroyed and how can any of you left behind go on without them. If you have lost your best friend you may feel there will never be anyone ever again in whom you can confide. We all ask ourselves *how will we survive*? It doesn't matter whom it was that you lost; you might feel an identity crisis in some form. Our loved ones can never be replaced but we can develop new and different relationships that bring us happiness.

In one of my counseling sessions my therapist said: "You will be happy again but you will never be so innocent and trusting. You will never know anyone who will love you the way Steve did. You may meet someone to love and be loved by, but you will then be a different person. You will never be able to repeat what you had with Steve. You might as well stop looking. The only place to find happiness is within you." She was absolutely right. We shouldn't try to replace our loved one, if we do that it is a form of denial and ultimately will keep us from moving forward. We must look within ourselves first for our happiness and once we do we have the ability to share our love in a healthy way. When we truly love ourselves we can begin to attract loving relationships into our lives.

We have all been changed because of what has happened to us and we must move forward in our new existence. I believe the grieving process allows us to find our new identity and that is when it is acting as our friend. It allows us to discover new aspects of our character that we may never have known existed. It really boils down to one thing and that is: Who do you want to become now that your life has abruptly changed? Do you want to find inner peace and happiness? What do you really want in your life? It is up to each person to begin making choices that lead them to find those answers.

Most of the roles we acquire in life allow us a chance to prepare in advance for them. For example, when we get engaged or married we plan those events far in advance. An expectant mother has nine months to prepare for motherhood. A new employee gets trained for his or her new job. In those situations we have had time to get our mind ready for the new experience. But when suicide occurs we have had no warning to the new status that has been imposed upon us and we often fall into a state of confusion. Initially I had no idea what my identity was without my husband. We were *soulmates* and our lives were tightly enmeshed. If I didn't begin to create a new identity for myself I would have never moved forward and ultimately stayed miserable.

Creating a new identity takes time. It doesn't happen overnight. You first must acknowledge that all those roles you played no longer exist. Or at a minimum they will be changed. Then you must be *OK* with not being in them and then discover what new ones you want to create for yourself. Once I accepted my status as a widow and not as a married woman I took off my wedding ring. The act symbolized my new identity to the world. It took me six months and when I did it I became open to new and different relationships to enter into my life. I slowly became a confident woman living on her own. My new attitude helped me move forward.

I also had to accept that I was no longer the wife of a politician. I could have stayed involved in the world of politics and rubbed elbows with the politicians but I chose to remove myself from all its activities. It freed me to devote my time to other interests. I began to do things for myself that would nourish my soul. I did things I enjoyed, such as bike riding, yoga and dancing. I allowed new things to enter my life and new doors continued to open for me. It is a process and it takes time, but if you are willing and believe in it, then things will happen for you as they did for me. The universe does not play favorites.

About eight months after Steve died I resumed dancing, although not the west coast swing dance I had done when he was alive. Instead I decided to try a new one. I chose Argentine Tango. It felt good to discover something new and it was tango that eventually led me to find love again. In the beginning new things are painful because they lead us into unfamiliar territory and take us out of our comfort zone. But as time passes we begin to feel more at ease with making decisions and learn to trust ourselves, thus paving the way to create a new identity.

Questions:

1) List the roles you played in the relationship to your loved one.

2) Have you accepted that you no longer have those roles?

3) List ways that you have created a new identity.

4) How does your new identity feel to you? Explain each of them.

5) If your new identity is not satisfying then write down the reasons why.

6) List what you will do to make them satisfying.

Chapter 7: Choices

I have learned that choice is a God-given gift and every one of them we make creates something negative or positive in our lives. When we are grieving it is very easy to make choices that are not healthy for us. We often want a quick relief to ease our pain. We drink too much or use drugs to numb ourselves so we don't feel the pain, but this is not a long-term solution. There are many other vices we use such as buying things with money that we may not have or finding ourselves in unhealthy sexual and non-sexual relationships. These may temporarily give us a *high* and make us believe that we are experts at handling our loss. But the truth is that masking the pain is only a Band-Aid and not a good long-term solution. We will never get to a healthy place if we are not willing to do the work. It takes a conscious awareness to begin the process. I began mine by going to a therapist and then finding a suicide support group. My therapist helped me see that some of my choices were not good for me.

I also learned that it was a choice to forgive myself, which I had not done. If we want to find peace in our life it is important that we forgive our loved one and ourselves. Without forgiveness there is no peace. Instead there is a constant battle within our heart. We must learn to forgive ourselves fully. Once we do then unconditional love flows freely. We can love ourselves when we have done something good and also when we have made mistakes. I don't like the word *mistake* because it is filled with negative energy and imposes blame. Can you change your belief system about mistakes and view them as lessons? Forgiveness for what you called *mistakes* is a necessary step in recovery.

The suicide group I attended created a safe environment for me to share my grief and not feel judged by anyone. We all gathered together for the same reason so I knew they could understand how I felt. I surrounded myself with people who encouraged me, not those who didn't offer hope and dragged me down. Choosing whom you spend your time and energy with will either help you move forward or hold you back. The choice is absolutely up to you and every one you make creates a consequence. You should ask yourself these questions before making them. Will this choice bring me closer to the person I want to become in my recovery? Will it benefit others or myself? Or will it hurt or cause harm? You must listen for the answer and the results will define who you really want to become.

I don't believe I really understood the *power of choice* until after Steve died. When he was alive, either he made the final decision or we discussed and made them together. Without him I had to learn to make them alone and I recognized the capacity they held to change my life. If I made a wrong choice, I could not hold Steve or anyone else responsible. It was all my doing. It forced me to think more clearly and prayerfully about them and at the same time I felt empowered knowing that I was creating my new story. I was going to be sure that my new one would be filled with purpose, gratitude, joy and love.

Questions:

1) List the negative choices you made as you dealt with your grief. Did you use drugs, alcohol or sex? Be honest, only you will see the answers.

2) Did you get negative affects from your choices?

3) Did your negative choices affect anyone else?

4) Are you happy about those negative choices?

5) List the choices you made that were good for you.

6) How did they make you feel?

7) Do you continue to make positive choices? If yes, write them down. If no, then why not?

Chapter 8: Staying on the Path of Recovery

I have come to realize that I am on a life long journey of recovery. Many people don't want to do the recovery work because it is hard to face their feelings and just "be" with them. It is an uncomfortable process, but one that is necessary if we want to move forward. Staying on the path means that you must check in with yourself to see how you are doing. Are you offering enough self-care? Do you have an attitude of gratitude? Do you offer praise to yourself for your accomplishments? Do you keep negative thoughts from controlling you? If not, it's important to get back on track and begin doing those things.

I have learned that there are many things in our life that can trigger our emotions and cause us to fall into a negative place. After Steve died I could not listen to Beatles music without crying. Steve was an avid guitar player and as a fan of the Beatles he often played their music. If a song came on the radio I had to turn it off because it evoked too much pain. Now I react much differently. In fact when a song comes on I feel a wonderful peace and Steve's presence. Another trigger for many women are hormones. We must recognize that during the times they are activated we can become extremely emotional and negative and fall back into grief.

We all have our own individual triggers that evoke negative emotions. It is important to begin to create positive triggers to replace the negative ones. They can be as simple as playing soothing music or dancing around the room, but stop whatever it is you are doing when they enter in and do something different and positive. A woman I know created a *joy jar.* She filled it with pieces of paper with things written on it that she was grateful for and when negative thoughts crept into her mind she randomly pulled out a message. It always changed her attitude to positive. My personal joy jar consists of: dancing tango, listening to the sound of ocean waves, snapping a photo of a sunrise or sunset, hearing good news from a friend, creating a meal for family or friends, calling someone I haven't spoken to for a long time, and the list goes on. It is important to incorporate your own jar of joys into your life.

Our journey gets easier when we realize that each person chooses to live their lives based on their own terms and who they desire to be, just as we live ours. We must relinquish all control over another human being, which helps keep guilt away. If we begin to lose sight of this then we can fall back on our journey.

Too many times we try to coerce people or use force to try to get what we want in life, but this is not allowing the other person to live fully. We must release controlling thoughts and actions and focus on things that will bring good into our lives. What we give energy to in our thoughts will expand so it is important to think on things that you want to bring into your life. If you are constantly thinking of miserable things, then misery is what you will attract. The old saying is true: misery loves company. So when negative thoughts bombard your mind it is important to recognize it and remove them quickly. I often say, "Cancel that thought." It helps me become aware that the thought is not edifying and serves no productive purpose.

Another thing that I believe is important is to create a peaceful environment in your home. Many times we turn on the TV and it evokes negative emotions. Be aware of this and turn it off when it happens and do something to change your mood. It is also important to have your surroundings pleasing to you. Is your home cluttered? Maybe it is a good time to declutter. Can you add some art that makes you feel good? I have very colorful pictures in my home because it arouses my creative spirit. The last piece I bought is in my bedroom and it is the first thing I see when I open my eyes. It is the creation of a young artist from Ireland named Mazer. It has geometric symbols with the colors: blue, purple, orange, and yellow. On one end there is an image of a torso with a fist and a leg that looks like it is kicking. On the other there is a torso and a leg that looks like it is running. When I saw it I interpreted it as a symbol for recovery. When we get kicked down in life, we get ourselves up and keep moving. That has been my life story. It's in my face every day and keeps me on my journey. You can find your own meaningful symbols to keep you on yours.

What also helps me stay on my path is to say positive words out loud because I believe that those energetic vibrations surround me wherever I am. Even if you don't believe the things you say it is important to say them anyway, such as *I am happy* or *love is coming to me now.* Say whatever you need in that moment. I have created 90 days of affirmations in chapter 10 for you to say out loud. This is an aid to help you revamp your life. The words you speak will begin to take on a life of their own and you will notice a change in your attitude. This will cause you to make more positive choices, thus you keep moving forward. You will soon discover that you are attracting positive people into your life. I have daily affirmations that I say and write them on Post-it notes and paste them in various locations that are easily visible. It is a way to keep my mind focused on the good.

As you travel on your journey you must persevere. This means to maintain the ability to endure, to carry on, continue in the same state without weakening or perishing. It is to go on in the face of pain, oppression, discouragement or suffering without being defeated. Those who are strong will run even faster when the kicks in life come their way. Remember that persevering in recovery takes continuous work. Over time, your persistence will bear fruit and you will have eyes to see beauty all around you. You will begin to look at life differently. You may see things that you have never seen before such as a butterfly fluttering around your window or colorful leaves blowing frantically on the ground in autumn. Accept it as a gift and one to be greatly treasured. If you do so then more and more beauty will appear in your sight. This doesn't mean that challenges will not enter into your life. But you will no longer let them take over and control you or rob you of your journey.

I believe we are all on our own sacred paths. Each of us has been changed by our tragedy. How could we not be? Yet, we have the opportunity to grow, discover, transform and always expand our ideas of what is possible. We can learn to see more clearly and deeply and learn to trust our intuition. We are courageous as we take each step along our path. Believe that you are exactly where you are meant to be in this moment. No matter what has happened in your past you can begin to shape your life story into a magnificent tale of triumph, courage, beauty, wisdom, power, dignity and love.

As the years race past, you can look back and reflect on your strength that brought you to where you are today. Stay strong, it is worth it in the end. I found happiness again so I know it is possible.

Questions:

1) List what you have done to stay on your path of recovery.

2) Can you build more ways into your life to stay on the path? List them.

3) Can you help others on their journey? How?

4) Have circumstances caused you to stray from the path? List them.

5) Make a list of things you are grateful for.

6) Create your own *joy jar.*

7) Reflect on your life and write down your strengths that brought you to where you are today.

Chapter 9: My Spiritual Transformation

This is the most important and exciting chapter for me. I believe the tragedy and grief I suffered are the reasons for my transformation. It has been a culmination of a long-awaited search. I have always been a *seeker* in my life. In other words wanting a connection to God and in search of higher truths. I often thought of myself as a Christian mystic. I went through periods when I was in and out of various Protestant church denominations, sometimes feeling connected to God and other times not. During my marriage to Steve I experienced a new level of spirituality. I had a deeper connection to God and to Steve because we shared mutual beliefs. There was an essence of true oneness between us.

Steve came to the knowledge that he needed God in his life and I did too. We lived our lives with God in our hearts and in our home. When Steve died by suicide I was thrown into a spiritual tailspin. I could not comprehend how a man who had faith in God could do such a devastating act. I questioned why the God we knew didn't protect him. I became angry with God for allowing it to happen and leaving me in such a horrible state. Initially I tried to push God out of my mind and heart during my grief.

I experienced the dark night of the soul and contemplated taking my own life so I could join Steve. But *truth* rose up from the pit of my being and I realized that I wanted to live. To do so, I first needed to forgive myself, God and Steve and then love myself unconditionally. This was not something that I was accustomed to doing and God's grace carried me and helped me to understand the profoundness of it. I went through a spiritual cleansing as I forgave myself for not being who I thought I should have been: the perfect wife, the perfect step-mom, the perfect church deacon, the perfect friend, the perfect neighbor, the perfect mother, the perfect child, the perfect daughter-in-law. Feeling like I hadn't met those expectations had caused self-loathing.

I slowly learned to be gentle with myself and grant myself forgiveness. I also needed to forgive Steve for ending his life and forgive God for feeling he had failed me. Once I did that the floodgates opened and I heard God's still small voice the same as I did at other times in the past. God never changed. It was me who did. I realized that I needed to go within and ask God to reveal all to me that had been stored deep in my subconscious mind that needed forgiveness. If you do this work you will be amazed what comes up. Things that you may have forgotten or haven't thought about in years will suddenly appear in your consciousness.

If we continue to harbor unforgiveness we potentially are robbed of health, prosperity, happiness and any peace of mind. Many philosophers and sages believe that our health is affected by our attitudes about others and ourselves. Forgiveness is the foundation to begin our healing.

A scripture verse that I had always used in times of stress returned to me: 2 Timothy 2:17. *For God gave us not a spirit of fearfulness; but of power and love and discipline.* (American Standard Version). I loved that verse because I knew God's power was ever present within me and I had nothing to fear for he would protect me. I have learned through all my pain and suffering that I have an incredible power within me. I have the power to heal my thoughts, make right choices, and to comfort others. I am a child of the magnificent God who created the universe and his power dwells within me and I can tap into it at any time. This power divinely directs me to greater truths.

I used many holistic modalities during my journey such as acupuncture, yoga, hypnotism, reiki, chakra healing, meditation and prayer. These all aided me in my healing and acceptance of who I was to become. I was evolving and opening my mind to God's living spirit of truth. After Steve died I stopped going to church. It was then that I realized I had a limited view of God and I had put him into a box. I had viewed him as a presence *out there* somewhere who answered my prayers if I followed all the rules, which I never could do. So I always carried guilt. I envisioned *Him* as sitting somewhere in the heavens favoring those who obeyed him and lived by all the religious rules. My ideas were tainted and engrained from their perspective. I knew there was something fallacious in my thinking but I would need to discover it for myself. It took all my suffering and pain for me to desire a spiritual enlightenment. It wasn't something that a church could teach me; it was something to be experienced.

I stayed away from churches for four years and that is when my true enlightenment began. I am not recommending that process as a way to find your enlightenment, to make peace with God or start your recovery, but for me it was necessary. I needed to wash my mind from all prior thoughts and beliefs and begin anew. During that time I spent hours taking long walks on the beach going within and seeking God.

It was during those times I quieted my mind, removing all thoughts and beliefs and asked God to reveal himself to me. I heard his voice many times in many different ways. I felt his presence as I heard the crashing sounds of the waves along the seashore, and felt his presence as the sand caressed my toes and the breeze brushed my arms. His presence was everywhere. God was in everything. He was in the very wave that I watched roll onto the shore. There was no place that God was absent. Why didn't I ever understand that truth before? It wasn't until I hit *bottom* that my spirit finally yearned for complete oneness with God. I felt re-born into greater awareness and this began my spiritual transformation. God helped me to see that many of the beliefs I held were false and I needed to re-evaluate how I viewed the world and all human beings.

This new awareness changed my thinking of how I viewed my own life. I was a person who suffered and survived a tragic loss. I began to understand that my life was a precious gift and meant to be lived to its grandest capacity. I have learned that each moment is to be savored even in the small mundane tasks, such as washing dishes or doing the laundry. Steve's suicide and my spiritual transformation have caused me to do things differently. I do everything in a *mindful* way believing there is purpose to every task and we can find joy in each one of them. I move more slowly and think more deeply about each action I take in life. I realize that each of us has a unique purpose no matter how large or how small. Mine is to encourage others. I can do this with my coaching services, the books I write and the posts on my Facebook page. I can also do it at the grocery store by holding a door open or helping an elderly person grab an item off the shelf. Doing simple acts of kindness give me purpose and can lead others to do the same.

After Steve's suicide I no longer believed in the permanence of anything anymore. Everything is a vapor and can dissipate in an instant. Therefore I cherish each and every moment. I consider every person I meet in life as a *holy encounter.* Even if the experience doesn't appear positive at the time, I believe that there are lessons to be learned and that the person entered my life for a reason. If there is a presence of negativity with the relationship it is important to not stay in it. I have learned to deflect negative energy and send the person off with a blessing. They too are a child of God and traveling on their own journey.

As God opened my eyes I became aware that I had been judgmental about many things and people. I may not have done it consciously but many times judged someone if they didn't fit into my mold or what I believed to be true. A perfect example is politics. Yes, we all have strong opinions, but who am I to say that I am right and someone else is wrong just because we think differently about issues? Another example is religion. Why should I determine who is righteous and who is not according to God? Many churches create an attitude of exclusivity. I have been to many that made it very clear that if you didn't believe as they taught then you would have no place in the kingdom of God.

I have come to realize that I am not the judge and try to live with a free spirit passing no judgments on anyone. This is not an easy thing to do in our society with all the information that is inundating our minds. One way that has made it easier for me is that I have removed myself from watching TV and listening to the news media. I don't let the opinions of others persuade me. I search for the truth and the answers from God. I don't feel as if I am missing out on anything. If something of importance has happened in the world God will make sure I find out about it.

As we continue to seek wholeness and seek God I believe that we will always have eye-opening moments. My experiences in life continue to build my faith and challenge me. One of my greatest has been with my writing. I started my memoir two years after Steve died and have worked on it for five years. I have tried to get it published but only received rejections. I have paid editors to help and became discouraged because I received opposing suggestions. I changed it several times based on their input and it became costly and frustrating. Many times I wanted to give up. My ego kept yelling at me loud and clear. I heard, "You're not a good enough writer, no one will want to read it. No publisher will pick it up. Do you really want to invest more money and self publish?" These negative thoughts circled in my head. I knew I couldn't allow them to stay. I canceled them and listened to the voice inside me that said, "The God source within has given you power. You have everything you need to accomplish your desires and they shall come to pass. You have a unique purpose and only you can write your message in a way that needs to be heard." I believe his message to be true so I continue to write. My soul is nourished and keeps me on my journey of recovery.

Each day is a new day to live and love and be thankful. I wake up every day and say, "Thank you God."

Stay on your journey of recovery.

Namaste,

~ Robin Chodak

Questions:

1) Have you had a spiritual transformation or any transformation? If so, list the ways you have changed.

2) Have others commented on your change?

3) Do you desire change?

4) List the things you can do to begin your change.

Chapter 10: 90-day inspirations

I have created 90 days of positive affirmations for you to read. These are simple, yet powerful phrases. I challenge you to begin a new habit of thinking positive for the entire 90 days. Each day read the affirmation out loud. Write down the affirmation and carry it with you. Even if you don't believe it still say it. It is important to let the sound vibrations surround you. There is power in the words. Memorize the phrase and let it fill your mind throughout the day or refer to your note. If the affirmation asks you to do something, *do it.*

If any negative thoughts enter your mind, then immediately remove them. After 90 days you will feel more positive and you will notice that you have filled your mind with less negativity. Keep this practice for the rest of your life. This is your journey to recovery.

Day 1 ~ I am a divine creation of God.

Day2 ~ I deserve to be happy.

Day 3 ~ I expect good to come into my life today.

Day 4 ~ I will remain calm today, no matter what circumstances arise.

Day 5 ~ I will not try to control another human being today.

Day 6 ~ I look at my image in the mirror and I say, "I am beautiful."

Day 7 ~ I am grateful today for __________. Fill in the blank.

Day 8 ~ Today I have everything I need.

Day 9 ~ Today I know that I am loved. I love myself.

Day 10 ~ Today I let go of all my worries and I let God take them.

Day 11 ~ I do not remember my mistakes. They are only lessons.

Day 12 ~ Today I open my mind to receive divine ideas.

Day 13 ~ I look out my window and I see beauty.

Day 14 ~ I forgive ________ today. Fill in the blank.

Day 15 ~ I am surrounded with pure, positive potential.

Day 16 ~ Nothing is impossible for my life.

Day 17 ~ I will say something positive to someone today.

Day 18 ~ I am healthy; each cell in my body is perfectly whole.

Day 19 ~ I release any anger that I am holding onto today.

Day 20 ~ Guilt will not control me today.

Day 21 ~ Today is a gift from God.

Day 22 ~ I am growing spiritually everyday.

Day 23 ~ I start this day with enthusiastic expectancy.

Day 24 ~ Happiness is my birthright.

Day 25 ~ I am filled with God's power.

Day 26 ~ I forgive myself for past errors.

Day 27 ~ I will inspire others today.

Day 28 ~ Today is filled with wonderful surprises.

Day 29 ~ I am perfect and whole just as God created me.

Day 30 ~ Today I speak only the truth.

Day 31 ~ Everything in my life works for my highest good.

Day 32 ~ My life is filled with adventure.

Day 33 ~ I love that my mind is filled with positive thoughts.

Day 34 ~ I will say a prayer for someone today.

Day 35 ~ Today I will tell someone I love them.

Day 36 ~ I will do something good for myself today.

Day 37 ~ I will do something good for a friend.

Day 38 ~ I will say a kind word to a stranger today.

Day 39 ~ I am filled with pure joy today.

Day 40 ~ I will quiet my mind for 10 minutes today.

Day 41 ~ I attract positive people into my life.

Day 42 ~ I know God has prepared good things for me today.

Day 43 ~ Today I release any shame that I carry.

Day 44 ~ I will smile often today.

Day 45 ~ I live in the absence of fear.

Day 46 ~ Others are attracted to my positive energy.

Day 47 ~ I am the creator of my reality.

Day 48 ~ I will do my best today.

Day 49 ~ I will not place blame on anyone today.

Day 50 ~ I accept the good into my life today.

Day 51 ~ I am pure positive energy.

Day 52 ~ I listen to the still small voice today.

Day 53 ~ I will laugh today.

Day 54 ~ I dream big things for my life today.

Day 55 ~ I will take a walk outdoors and observe nature.

Day 56 ~ I choose to be happy today.

Day 57 ~ My creativity is at its peak today.

Day 58 ~ I will not be discouraged today.

Day 59 ~ I exude confidence today.

Day 60 ~ I bask in God's love today.

Day 61 ~ I am filled with joy.

Day 62 ~ I live a life of abundance.

Day 63 ~ I learn something from every experience.

Day 64 ~ I manifest good into my life.

Day 65 ~ I am a wise soul.

Day 66 ~ I deny the appearance of evil.

Day 67 ~ I am filled with strength.

Day 68 ~ I am filled with God's light.

Day 69 ~ I am glad to be alive today.

Day 70 ~ I am open to God's truth.

Day 71 ~ I am prosperous in all things.

Day 72 ~ I expect the best of everything today.

Day 73 ~ I will not re-visit yesterday.

Day 74 ~ I will celebrate this day.

Day 75 ~ I can accomplish all I put my mind to do.

Day 76 ~ My desires are satisfied.

Day 77 ~ I have loving relationships.

Day 78 ~ I eliminate all negativity from my life.

Day 79 ~ I will have no doubt in my life today.

Day 80 ~ I walk in faith today.

Day 81 ~ I will not coerce another human being.

Day 82 ~ I view every person as God's creation.

Day 83 ~ I will exercise for 30 minutes today.

Day 84 ~ I will put only healthy foods into my body today.

Day 85 ~ The word boredom is not in my vocabulary.

Day 86 ~ The universe responds to how I feel today.

Day 87 ~ I confidently expect to succeed today.

Day 88 ~ I am important to God.

Day 89 ~ I am important to others.

Day 90 ~ I send out love into the universe today.

Now, how do you feel? Have you noticed a change in your thought patterns? Keep saying these affirmations over and over again and create some of your own. They are limitless. If you do this you will create your new positive identity.

Chapter 11: Meditation

This book is the result of my participation in a group meditation so I will end it with one for you. Not surprisingly, the idea to do so came during another group meditation.

Meditation has helped me greatly on my journey. When I need guidance from my higher source (God) then I meditate and wait for the answer. It always comes. It may not be the one I think it should be, but it will come. As you meditate begin to trust yourself and trust your source. If you are not familiar with the practice the only thing you need to do is close your eyes and pay attention to your breath. Breathe in and breathe out with a slight exhale. If your mind wanders come back to your breath. Read the meditation I wrote and let the words comfort you and allow your mind to quiet. You can also record the words and listen to them with your eyes closed.

Meditation:

Gently take a deep breath in, hold it for five seconds, and then exhale through your mouth slowly. Repeat this three or four times. Imagine yourself standing on a beach looking at the vast blue ocean. Feel the expansiveness of your surroundings. Notice how the white caps gently roll onto shore and then dissipate into nothingness. Watch as it happens over and over again. Continue to watch for several minutes until you are mesmerized from the movement of the waves and the sound as they come towards your feet. Feel the sand under your toes. A wave rises up to your ankles and you feel the warm water caress your feet.

You close your eyes and you feel the warm sunshine on your face. You feel the presence of serenity that you have never felt before. You hear a voice that says, "I am with you always. Let go of all your fears and anxieties." You feel more and more relaxed and you realize you are in the presence of pure being. You feel empowered and know that "All is well." You bask in the comforting presence for several minutes. You gently open your eyes and the words flow easily from your mouth out towards the ocean. "I will live my life to its highest potential. I have the power within to accomplish everything I need." You take a deep breath and you are hopeful and refreshed. You know that you want to experience this peace again. And you shall.

I hope that this book has inspired you and given you hope no matter where you are on your journey.

Love and light,

Robin Chodak

If you are interested in coaching sessions contact me through my website.

http://robinchodak.com/coaching-sessions-robin-chodak/

Certified Grief, Life, Spiritual Coach

Certified Master NLP (Neuro-Linguistic Programming) Practitioner

ABOUT THE AUTHOR

Robin Chodak is a survivor of her former husband's suicide in 2005. She has been transformed and found purpose and passion in her life by helping others who suffer from grief. She is a certified grief, life and spiritual coach and a certified master NLP (Neuro-Linguistic Programming) practitioner. She offers one-on-one coaching at www.robinchodak.com

Robin has created a Facebook page for survivors www.facebook.com/recovernowfromloss.

Her publications include, "Love Will Go On", in *The Daily Word* September/October 2016 issue, "There is Hope for Your Journey", *SOSBSA (Survivors of Suicide Bereavement Support Australia),* "Personal Survivor Story", *Catholic Charities Loss (Loving Outreach to Suicide Survivors),* "Surviving after Loss", in *AFSP(American Foundation for Suicide Prevention)* and a contributor in Tom Sweetman's Book: *From Grief to Greatness* and Matlida Butlers's Book: *Tales of Our Lives: Fork in the Road.*

Robin's other passion is dancing Argentine Tango. It was the catalyst to meeting her second soulmate, Dr. Gerald Chodak whom she married on 11-11-11.

She and her husband live the winter months in Highland Beach, Florida and the summer months in Michiana Shores, Indiana. They are blissfully happy!

50146789R00064

Made in the USA
Columbia, SC
03 February 2019